about the author

Taryn Riddle is a young American poet interested in mental illness and wellness. Taryn was raised in Bolton, Massachusetts and practiced daily journaling from the time she could first hold a pencil through her early college years. Her writing is inspired by personal struggles and life experiences. At the time of this publication, she resides in Boston, Massachusetts and is a recent college graduate with a bachelor's of science in behavioral neuroscience and philosophy. Taryn is active on social media, most notably on Instagram @tarynriddlee.

All illustrations for this book are by Taryn Riddle.

dedication

for anyone who is afraid to fall asleep.

*i hope that in reading this book
you may feel less alone.*

Taryn Riddle

SOMNAMBULIST CHRONICLES

AUSTIN MACAULEY PUBLISHERS®

LONDON · CAMBRIDGE · NEW YORK · SHARJAH

Ordering information
Quantity sales: Special discounts are available on quantity purchases by corporations, associations, and others. For details, contact the publisher at the address below.

Publisher's Cataloging-in-Publication data
Riddle, Taryn
Somnambulist Chronicles

ISBN 9798889105879 (Paperback)
ISBN 9798889105886 (ePub e-book)

Library of Congress Control Number: 2023924706

www.austinmacauley.com/us

First Published 2024
Austin Macauley Publishers LLC
40 Wall Street, 33rd Floor, Suite 3302
New York, NY 10005
USA

mail-usa@austinmacauley.com
+1 (646) 5125767

content warning

This book contains or references the following themes:

Abusive relationships, blood, bullying, cheating in romantic relationships, death, depression, eating disorders, knives, mental illness, misogyny, pregnancy, profanity, PTSD, rape, self-harm, sexual assault, sexually explicit wording, slut-shaming, and suicidal ideation.

These can be sensitive topics and are not intended for everybody. Reader discretion is kindly advised. Thank you for reading!

table of contents

the incident

this is the part
where a youthful romance
turns dark: like our minds
it comes with age, they say

when boyfriend and girlfriend
war for peace, but war wins
i promise i didn't see it coming

and because of that
i will skip to the part
that was unexpected

the hard part
when things went downhill
and i fell

the sleepiest flower
she fell, not in love
she fell, *like dusk*

and so, he picked her:
the prettiest flower
of everything that lives;
and that was the moment
she stopped growing.

i honestly never thought
to look down
until a boy from school
pointed between my legs.

i look down
between my legs
but i have no authority
no power

only pink chaos.

prickly pear
chartreuse and flowering and ripe
oh, how god frowns
as your pubescent hairs
are grazed by the lips
of strange men
but oh, *why then,*
did he make you that way?

i do not like the way
older men look at me like i am
fresh meat off a forbidden green apple,
candy toffee, sugar lips—

no thank you, sir…
oh honey
i said no thank you, sir.

and he teased
i have demons
if you want to see them
i said no, thanks
i am already battling my own

remember not to get
too close
to stars
like hearts
they're all just little
flaming rocks

have you ever been told
wow, you have been through a lot;
i want to show you what real love is.

by a man who proceeds
to crumble you worse
than anyone ever before him.

but falling in love can be a painful experience, too. every
ounce of yourself that you give to somebody else: you no
longer have as your own. i have made the mistake many
times of picking myself to pieces, giving each one away,
and finding myself broken in the end.

like a statue that is chipped away at
until the face is no longer distinguishable.
until it could no longer be considered art.

and when people leave you (because inevitably, they may),
you will find that you know nothing of who you are
anymore. i know you love this person. i know you want to
give yourself away to somebody who will cherish it with all
the hopefulness of childhood.

but remember to sustain yourself, too:
for such a loss is the price you pay for adoration.

so, if it is really an act of self-destruction,
it can no longer be considered love.

i feel more alone with you
than i did when i used to be
actually alone

please just tell me
i am the most beautiful
you've ever had.

what is worse
than going to bed angry?

you allowed me
to fall asleep at night
in your bed, for god's sake,
wondering if i was good enough.

and he told me
go ahead, leave me

you will not find anyone else who can love you:
you are not pretty enough

a thousand mattresses could not mask
the indent of a tiny pea
which exists, audaciously, in her bed
despite months of starvation

—the princess and the pea

tell me that you love me
not because you do
but because i need
your *sweet nothings*
just to stay alive.

how funny it is
that people can go
from best friends,
to lovers, to broken pieces
and back again
all within a matter of days.

you wouldn't know this because i keep everything bottled up. but if you would open me up, you would be surprised to find a hundred tiny soldiers. they'd run in all directions like a colony of spiders set free from the traps of a glass mason jar. each of them represents one small battle i have swallowed. snippy comments, insecurities, and full-blown arguments. count them, and you will realize the wear and tear you've accumulated inside me. just wait, because someday i will break and you will be swarmed by the wrath of my resentment. because the thing is, you are both the war and the prize. and you may think you like trojans, but you haven't met the horse.

i am your trojan horse.

and that is the thing about codependency. everyone else wants something easy, something comfortable. but me? i want to kiss the wounded parts of you. i want to witness every crying spell so violently felt. the essence of human emotion: so vivacious, so that even the people around us could palpably feel the passion between us. i want to embrace your soul, hold it tender, and tell it that *i know you hurt from things you don't talk about.* but *things will be okay.* and that *broken things make better art.* there is so much beauty in being imperfectly human, and that is so much more attractive than anything reminiscent of perfection or ease.

—i want to feel the pain, the good pain.

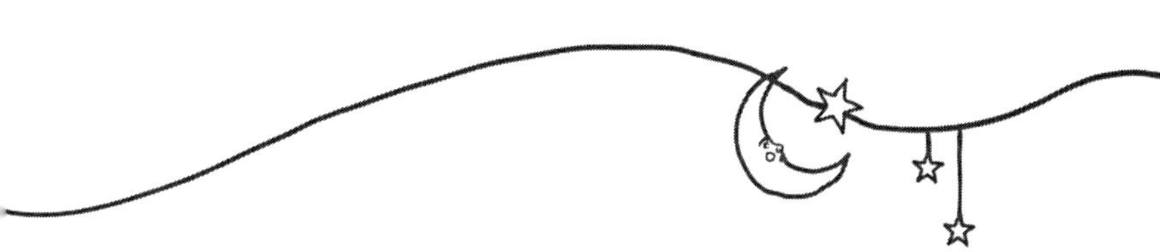

so what if i was the first
to bring a blade to my wrist?

you were the first
to twist the knife.

you know what hurts more than crying in a bathroom? crying in your boyfriend's bathroom. because he gets angry when you cry in front of him. he does not understand why i do it. he does not know i am trying to molt the layer of me that loves him back. i spend hours working up the courage to leave him, just to back out halfway through the conversation. he promises he will change, but he does not even know what the definition of change is. and every time he again fails to learn, i find myself in the same cycle again. crying in his bathroom: shedding the aspects of my personality i used to love about myself. picking myself apart trying to find scraps of myself that agree with him. because i refuse to admit that i am not the one for him.

it's funny.
you said you'd kill me
for leaving you
but now you don't have to

because i cannot bring myself to leave you
and i am already dying inside.

and he said

                    if you take me for granted
                 i will take everything from you;

i have done it before.

and just like that
this is the part
where i was taught a new meaning
for the phrase *sleeping together*
to be fair, i did not know much of it
by the time of the incident;
however, i had experienced sex before
but never like this.
i am not so sure, looking back,
that sex was the right word for it
because i thought that *sex*
was supposed to be between
two or more people
not one person and one body
and i thought that *sex*
was supposed to be between
two or more people
who wanted *sex* to happen.
but this. this was none of that.
i think there is a better word for this.
one letter longer than *sex*.
i will type is as a whisper
so please whisper in your mind
when you read it

r a p e

you have to make it a slow burn.
salty tears streaming down the side of your face,
you are lying on a pillow facing the wall,
away from your boyfriend.
slow breaths so as not to make a sound.
you want to shudder. moan. heave. sob.
you want to water the flowers.
but you need to let it out slowly. gently.
like plucking a dandelion,
make it a gentle, soft death.
let it down slowly. so slowly
that you fall asleep.

to be truly young
is to lose it
before noticing.

she just lay there, motionlessly, as it happened. pervasive thoughts rubbing against the private tissues of her mind, swarming about her hair and neck like bees and draping her face in soft white honey. and she breathed. air moved in and out, in and out, in and out of her, as she breathed. but she wouldn't open her eyes. she couldn't. behind the thinness of her eyelids, she saw only darkness: a pitch-black nighttime construct of her own cerebrum. stars flickering about like miniature fireworks inside her brain as the daytime outside moved on without her. and she just existed there, floating in time, as it happened.

for a long time, i had this sinking feeling that something bad happened to me. but i could not put my finger on it. it left a bad taste in my mouth and i could not stop wondering about it. but my brain locked away the memory and threw out the key. that's called 'repressed memory'. but without the memory, my suspicion was as thick as fiction. eventually, i gave up on the idea that something was even wrong. because no matter how hard i tried, i could not remember anything. and soon after i gave up was when it finally hit me. the big, bad, terrible thing. and it was indeed terrible: it was exactly as i had suspected.

—damn you, repressed memory.

no, i do not remember everything
but i remember how i felt in that moment
when my eyes shot open, limbs still heavy
from the chains of drowsiness.
and i sat up in bed; told you to get off me

and never spoke of it again.

walk fast on lonely streets
with keys between knuckles
hesitantly peer over your shoulder
and pray there is not a man there

—life of woman

you can leave
but you'll never escape me anyway:

i took your virginity
and you took mine.

—teenage fragility

-why i take iron supplements-

why do i ingest supplemental iron each night before bed? why add one more pill to my already-heavy drug regimen? why at twenty-one years old? because at seventeen, my anemia forced me to become vulnerable. at an already-vulnerable age: my teens. i used to pass out often; in class, while driving, anywhere and any time that my body felt the burden of consciousness was too great to bear. the omnipotence of my anemia felt heavier than even the thickest and strongest sleeping syrups. day after day, i let the crushing weight of sleepiness besiege me. but even that hellishness is not why i take iron supplements. i take iron because i am afraid that boys my age will touch me while i am unconscious. i am afraid that grown men will make alive my body while my brain is dead to the world. because it has happened before. i take iron supplements because i need to feel in control of my own body again. despite the deep cuts left over on my shins after a full day of wearing socks. despite my purple fingertips in february temperatures. despite chronic fatigue and even depression. *here i rise.* i cannot control the past, but i will shape the future with my fear: the fear that inspires my drive to not let the rape happen ever again. maybe not at seventeen, but at twenty-one, i will raise all of hell before a man takes anything from me. especially something i *already lost* at seventeen. i will be nobody else's. i will be *woman.* and yes, i may be anemic. but i must not be vulnerable.

who was your rapist?
they ask,
expecting someone evil.

but no,
he was the first boy
i ever loved.

tough sleeper
i've slept through fire alarms

but one day awoke
to you inside me

slept through the rape
oh, why

sound sleeper
no sound sleep

somebody tell me
what is the difference between
being unconscious and falling asleep?

is it the brain waves that
scribble across paper like
the thin white lines that
stripe your arms?

is it the pale pink of
sleeping flesh not pale enough
to be without a soul?

is it the heartbeat beating
or pillows for lungs
gently rising and falling inside
the hollow of your ribs like
butterfly eyelids that flutter
when we dream?

somebody tell me
why depression makes us sleepy
beyond all childhood tiredness
or thick sleeping syrups
as we spend our lonely days
in blissful unconsciousness?

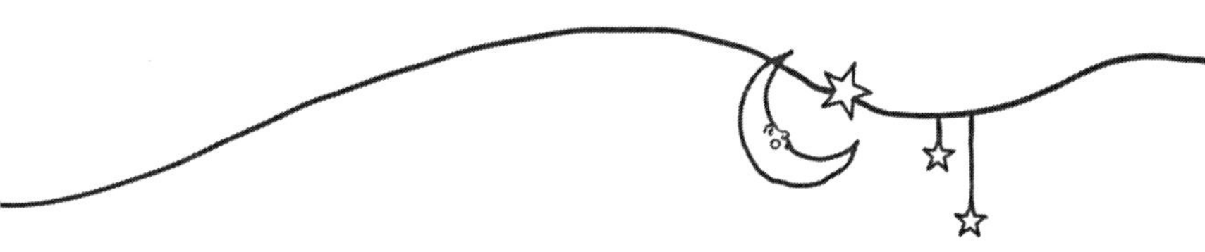

sleep, coma
yin, yang
drunkard, soma
shower, rain

the only difference is consent.

you did not just pull the rug on me.

you stole the whole damn floor.

i miss trusting someone
with every ounce of my being
but after you, to be honest,
i do not think i ever will again.

i plucked every rose petal
from the apology bouquet
you bought for me

and i ate them.
i just do not believe
that you are sorry.

his hands were evergreen. they touched places only bullets
and god should touch. he made promises for things that
nobody should promise. and surprise, surprise: when he
finally broke them, he stuffed beheaded roses in my mouth.
the ones i bought from the pharmacy hoping money could
buy our relationship more time. they tasted the way
potpourri smells. i chewed them and spat them out.
everything strewn about the floor, i sunk my knees into the
mess of petals and burst into tears.

—i watered the flowers.

*eight billion souls on this planet
and yet, you do not have one*

oh, i looked up to you
taller than me
i thought you knew things

but in the end

you were only tall.

i thought i was hollow
before i met you
expecting you to fill me up
and i hoped you would fix
the holes in my heart
but in the end
you left me feeling
completely drained

—on emptiness

living inside her ears takes a toll
so many male lips
with aged beards, they whisper
unwarranted sweet nothings

their wrinkled mouths
over-enunciate catcalls
they leave tiny droplets
of spit on her face

grazing hands, uncalled for
raise the dead: the hairs on her neck
skin grows goosebumps
with rage, at their imbecility

such fools, foul, shoo
dear god, *if walls could talk*
they would speak the things
that women repress

because these men cannot stand the thought
of women who bleed.

four-dollar razor blades
and all *man* can think of
is that this is a new opening in my body
into which he may insert himself
and his opinions.

"you had everything"

predictable words from a man
who said i'd never find anything more

"you are not pretty enough"
"nobody will want you"

you tell me to smile
even after everything
i'll show you my teeth

big talk for a man
who my other exes refer to
as my rapist.

the aftermath

this is the part
where depression takes over
i am living on autopilot
i feel out of place
and yet i also feel
absolutely nothing at all
i continue to wonder
how depression makes us sleepy
a deep, heavy sleepiness
thicker than any sleeping syrup
sometimes i wonder
if this narcoleptic pattern
of falling asleep against my will
at school, while driving,
while sitting after a meal
is a way for my brain
(the brain that controls my body)
to save me from my own mind
(the mind that contains the darkness)

goodnight sky
goodnight rain
goodnight thunder
goodnight pain

sleep is freedom
from a violent consciousness

what is this 'sleep' you speak of?

in my dreams, i die each night
just to be resurrected
with the early dawn.

what is this 'end' you speak of?

how will i know
on which morning
my sun will not rise?

can you count the stars?
that speckle dark skies endlessly
like the billions of tiny neurons
fueling my mental illness?
countless grains of sand upon the earth's surface
or endless variations of macronutrients
to make up a day of eating?

when you begin to count them,
do you start to feel sick the way i do?
a sinking feeling in your stomach
that in all the universe's infinity,
your existence is completely meaningless.

starlight
star bright
i wish that i could sleep tonight
wish i may
wish i might
not wake up in tears tonight.

stars fight
stars might
throw their sparks and stones
starry blithe
star-shaped kite
you break my fucking bones.

starlight
you are bright
like the first boy i ever loved
wish i may
wish i might
fall asleep at last, with you above.

you know what i feel like?

single stars in blue skies

out of place

and awake at the wrong hours.

i feel as though i am sleepwalking
through life:

numb.

i just want to feel something.

champagne and cold caffeine

70

to feel alive again.

asleep with
my eyes open

the sickest i've ever been in my life
and yet perfectly able-bodied

dying inside
but somehow alive

you don't know pain
until you have begged on your knees
for a god you don't believe in
to heal you.

i am jealous of everyone who does not struggle to get out of bed in the morning, hungover from the previous evening's violent tantrums and crying spells and tired after constantly startling awake from night terrors. i am jealous of everyone who has friends, can reach out to people without feeling like a burden, and does not hate themselves. i am jealous of everyone not plagued by the energy-sucking inconvenience it is to be alive.

and if it weren't for
the hollow pang in my stomach
grounding me to my body
on sleepless nights,

i might wrongly assume
that i was never alive at all.

and here i am
here i fucking am
i find myself soapboxing
in the fetal position, lamenting
to the white acrylic pan
of a dormitory shower:

i don't want to be asleep forever
i'm just scared to be lonely

like how distant streetlights

blur together

because my eyes can't fucking see

why can i see the void?

open me up, and you will find
a bunch of dead wishes
and rusty pennies.

a childhood innocence
lost to the violent destruction
of heartbreak and starvation.

words on the rocks
tequila and a broken prayer

notebook secrets
shovel soil

dead penny wishes
lay here

we practice dying often:
when we refuse to write our books;
poetry is not a dead language, don't you know?
because poetry is alive and breathing.
it is a gutsy, ruptured-heart sort of thing.
and of poetry: do not attempt to read mine
with a weak stomach or a fear of blood.
the emotions i swallow and the words i bleed:
ink pools at the bird's bill if not held gently.
and although we are war-torn by love, in a
half-the-weight-i-used-to-be sort of way,
we must be soft. like-an-empath soft.
so even if our voices grow quiet over the years
from too many cigarettes, i'll still have
a nagging worry chewing on my ear.
the worry is that the noise in my head
will never age quietly. i cannot imagine
ever settling down. feeling calm.
content or peaceful, refined or behaved.
i am none of those things. so even if i were,
that is to say, a virgin: there is a child
who will outstay this little life of mine.
because if there ever was a true birthplace
for madness, it would be a poet's mind.

letters don't form words anymore.
just pockets of knowledge
too high up for little me
to reach, like a fresh apple
off the forbidden tree
(why is thinking easy for everyone but me?)
and i am drowning in oceans of
useless tissue, my parasitic brain

and i mouthed under my breath
where do memories go
when you forget them?
my voice shook as i asked,
but i will speak my mind
in the face of my brain.
she did not answer.

i whispered louder
where do memories go
when you forget them?
my brain cleared her throat:
they go back to where
they came from.

and where is that? i leaned in closer
i do so wish to find my youth again
and my brain rolled her eyes:
don't you know it's in the present?

and to think

i have played off
the lowest points of my life

by saying i was fine.

but not all men
but not all men
but not all men

insists the other man
insists the other man
insists the other man

why did i do it? *cheat?*
well, sometimes already-sexualized people
don't know how to express themselves
without using *sex*
and the cheating, as they call it
was my way of rebelling
it felt like nobody could hear my voice
muffled like underwater
maybe they just did not care
my 'friends' sure didn't
but i still had one thing
i could use to express myself
my sexuality, if you will
i think that is why
the phrase is coined *body language.*

i was so starved for connection
that i confused empathy
for romantic attraction.

this is the part
where i lost my friends
when the word got out
that i cheated on my boyfriend
my boyfriend [who raped me]
[correct: i did not break up with him for that]
because my friends do not stay friends
if one of us becomes a *slut.*

and how did i become a slut?
by cheating on him, of course.

and so, once again
my teddy bear and i
reunite as best friends
out of necessity.

—even sluts need teddy bears

and it is hard going to school every day,
acting as though everything is fine.
acting like i wasn't raped
in the first semester of senior year.
and yet, at the same time,
feeling like the world knows my secret.
feeling like people do not see me
as a person anymore.
i am just a feminine object.
i'm just a 'pretty' face stitched on
to an already-used seventeen-year-old body.

—beauty isn't much if it's all you're seen as.

they ask me how sure i am
of what he did
i say fucking crystal

and they still think i am lying.

people ask why i am so open
about my feelings and trauma.

and that makes me stop for a second.
and question myself. but honestly?

the world does not need any more
broken secrets or hushed voices.

i am standing here, naked.
for all to see.

and i will give everything i have to give:
because it is all i know how to do.

look at me or don't.

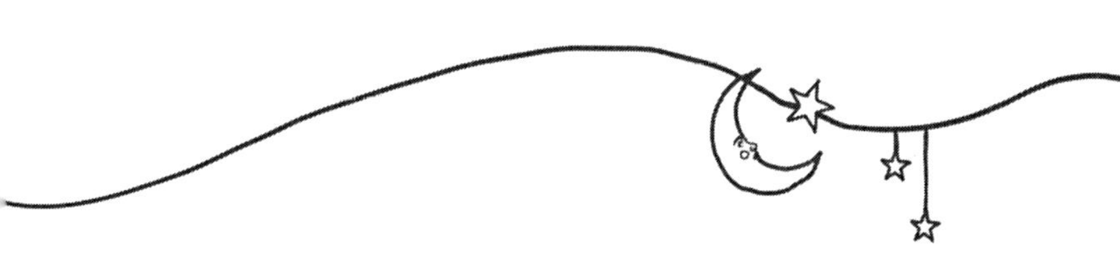

why do i talk about it?

because i am not the only one.

and i'll stop screaming

when they stop telling me it is in my head.

are my feelings
not valid enough
that i must also
provide a reason
for feeling so?

the lust between my legs
grows drier and colder
every time you tell me
the one thing
i always warn you not to say:

"you are overreacting"

does it count as rape
if i was drunk on self-hatred,
gastric acid, and actively bleeding
from the wrists?

what about if i was asleep?

it is hard to be the honest one
in a world that does not speak.

when the smoke clears
and it will

you will find that the mirror
has cracked

did i cheat

or did i just find
someone easier to trust?

i daydreamed weddings and futures into existence with only my mind: just short of magic, no? and the grooms were always people i'd wanted so badly to have significance in my life. but in the end, they were never more than just that: a daydream; a fantasy about the possibility of someone loving me. and in reality? they never wanted more than my body.

i wanted so badly
to be the exception.

the exception to the idea
that all that young men want

is women's bodies
but not the minds attached to them.

the exception to how he said
he was emotionally unavailable.

i thought i could change him.
i could stand out in a crowd.

if i was just *good enough.*

pretty enough.
charming enough.

but it turns out, i am not the exception.
i am not sure if there even is one.

does death lust for my soul
every time i fall asleep?

does she crave the taste of my blood
as much as surgical stainless?

does she miss me in the morning?
like how i wanted him to?

all i wanted
was to take back *control*
and they said i was a *slut*

tell me then, what about me,
specifically,
makes me a *slut?*

is it my insulted vagina
after what i knew
to be an after-school nap?

my mutilated arms:
tens of more openings
for men to insert themselves?

is it the non-consensual sex
or the persistent hope that
it's not all men?

the reflexive tendency
to look elsewhere for validation
after my boyfriend failed?

or is it just the misconception
that women are innately seductive
and therefore, *must be blamed?*

go tell them
i was the sweetest
girl you knew

and when they
don't believe you

be honest:
you were the one
who turned me bitter.

i live my life on the belief
that good people
are few and far between.
people call me *toxic*
because i draw them in
only to twist their words
and put them through
psychological warfare.
but i only do it
because i am afraid
of it happening to me.
i try to get ahead:
get them before they get you.

and i guess, at the time,
feeling like i *found* you
made up for the fact
that i *lost* things
along the way

—things like dignity and friends

my sweet mother said
we could invite *all* my friends
to my birthday party, but i said
mother, i have none.

only the most
warm-blooded of people
have the capacity to feel hurt
the way you and i do.
we are soft.
we are over-feelers.
we are empaths.

sitting all alone in the cafeteria,
i am not asking for pity.
but i wish somebody, anybody,
would notice me.

how does it feel,
not having any friends?
you never asked.

it's not like what you would think.
it sucks, but it's not sad.
it is a freedom so sweet
you wish you could share it
with someone— *oh*.

sometimes when i think about
the people who have hurt me

i wish i could talk with them
not because i want to face them

but because i would like to know
why

they stomp all over you
like salt and gravel
as if you deserve it
and the worst part is
you believe them.

the breakup

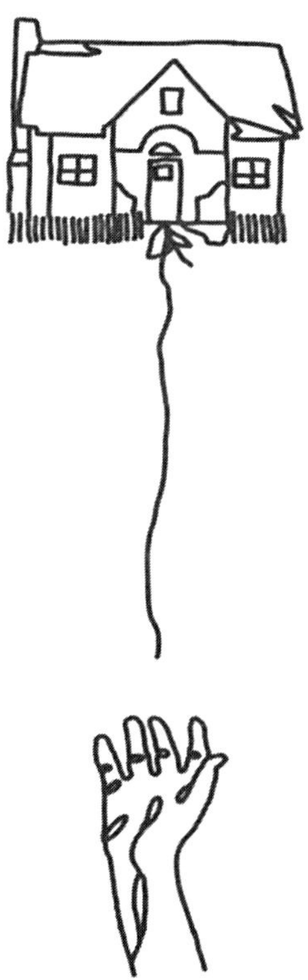

this is the part
where that boyfriend
i told you about
[that boyfriend who raped me]
and got away with it
believe it or not
he broke up with *me.*

and believe it or not
that hurt worse than the rape
worse than any of it:
the self-harm, the bullying, the verbal abuse.

he may have ravaged my body
senior year of high school.

but the breakup—
he destroyed my *heart*
freshman year of college.

you wrote to me in a love letter:

i keep falling for you, and the best part is
i don't think there will be a floor for me to hit.

hindsight's a bitch: it was a glass ceiling.

if you leave me
does that mean

my appeal
was only temporary?

'all good things must come to an end'
didn't know that applied to beautiful men

i suppose it would be *foolish*
to call our relationship 'good'
though all such things, indeed,
must come to a tragic end.

and i still feel like a fool.

i promised you
i'd never promise you anything

and here i am still:
a fool in the end.

because i never complained
about the broken bed
i never would have said anything
if you had not begun the dust-up
and despite cracks in the walls
creeks in the floorboards
you were always home to me.

but if i cannot be
the greatest love of your life

then i will be
the most tragic one who got away.

in the beginning,
you were sad for me
so you loved me extra hard
because you knew i needed it.

in the thick of it,
you became frustrated
that you could not fix me
despite giving me everything.

and in the end,
you were unapologetic:
breaking up with me, saying
go get a sharper knife.

—every love story that features
the girl with crimson wrists.

and the crimson molasses
pouring from open wounds;
let it be the syrup
that drowns every theory of us.

what if i only liked myself
because you liked me

and now that you don't want me
i don't want me

i used to to stay up late
nights talking on the phone
telling you things about me
that only god should know

did that mean nothing?

because it seems to me
that i gave up sleep
sweet, much-needed sleep
to talk to someone

who is nothing but a stranger now.

and the sad part is
you never even saw
the best of me.

i am a remnant
of my former self
because of you
and the worst part is
you don't even think of me.

you took me to the ocean
pointed to the skyline
where the two blues meet
and swore on water itself
that you'd never leave me.

and the sad part is?
i have no idea where you are
or what you are doing now.

how can you tell me
there are plenty
of fish in the sea
when everyone knows
the oceans are dying?

someday
i will not sob uncontrollably
when you double-cross my mind.

but for now,
i have to.

the butterflies my stomach used to hold for you are now dead and festering, their skeleton wings slowly being eaten away by decomposing fungi and little gnats. and the worst part of it all? the dead butterflies will not vanish quickly enough. even the circle of life cannot swallow you whole. there is too much of you. you are too damn special.

when we lose somebody we thought we were in love with, we start to grieve for the memories that never even happened. we miss the person we fell in love with in our heads. the life we imagined with them: fantasies of loving them. but in the end, none of that was real. we have always been just two high schoolers. we never had a family, even though we planned one. the house we would have someday; the pets we wanted to name. but no, none of that was ours. perhaps *we* were never even ours.

i know it will take a month or two to heal, but will i even last that long? my days are a balancing act between numbly, robotically going through the motions, barely conscious of time passing, and violent storms of my own decay where i find myself curled up on the shower floor begging god to drown me. if i could turn back time, i would find a way to not get to this point. *don't let this be the end.* i scream a childish scream that pierces the numbness and lifelessness of everything. and then i stop. because i am tired. so fucking tired that it's not consensual. it feels like the weight of the world is on my shoulders and i am begging my body to collapse. how many hospitalizations before i finally die? everything in me is fighting against the idea that this is my life now, but in reality, i am decaying every day from the pain. and even as i write this, the page blurs as my eyes fill with tears. and i want to keep going but there is nothing left in me to fight: except the secret worry that i will die for real if i think about him for more than a fleeting moment.

you always said
you would never give up on us

now you're just something
that i used to love

and i always say:
better to have loved and lost

—easier said when you're not shattered

they say smile
because it happened
but i'll cry for now

it feels like my body is rejecting the organs that once were mine, but you made yours. as they say: bad blood. the physical tearing, limb from limb; separating what is mine from what is yours. and the sad part is? you own more of me than me. the halves are not equal in the divorce. my stomach churning knives all the while; my arms hot from blood rushing to my extremities. my eyes glazing over until i blind myself with the pain of it all: a sudden and overwhelming disgust for the one person i wanted so badly to play a critical role in my life. and i guess, in the end, you did. but i was expecting white roses, flower girls, and ribbons. this: this is not that. this is the moment i have been dreading; the moment i had hoped i could avoid in my youth. the moment when i realize boys can enter my body but they should never own it. that when somebody becomes one with your soul, you must not lose yourself in the process. the old drag that individuals are mere halves of what they have yet to find *is wrong*. you are a whole person all on your own. do not do what i have done. do not shred yourself to pieces and leave a relationship knowing and having less than you entered in with.

—rage: the fear of unmet expectation

follow your heart

is what everyone
keeps telling me
but if mine is broken
into several pieces

which way do i go?

weeks and months later, still my
skin itches for a touch from yours
eyes lust for a single glimpse of you
lips starve for the taste of your mouth
and even as i know in my heart
that you do not want me anymore

my sobbing whisper shakes
please, tell me i'm wrong

why won't you leave?
my ex: i mean.
he is the monster under my bed.
he screams at me in the night:
it is loud inside my head.
the thought of someone
who i used to love with all my being
now nothing but a haunting image
of all my insecurities
from during our relationship
now finally achieved in their final form.
i used to sleep soundly in his arms.
i can no longer do that;
so now i have insomnia.
i've always slept with a teddy bear,
even as an adult;
perhaps, that is because
part of my adolescence
was taken. is incomplete.
and alas, here we are again:
just me and my teddy and my demons.

when we were in love, i used to lay on top of you: to hear your heart beating in your chest and feel the most at peace i've ever been knowing that it was beating for me.

but once you left me, i spent many nights curled up in the fetal position; alone in my bed that you made ours, except now it is just mine again… but it still feels like *yours*. and you slept underneath it. the monster under my bed, i mean: haunting every image of dreams i attempted to dream without you. but the reality is that i do not want a life without you in it.

and i wish i could work up the courage to crouch down and pull you out from under the bed: beg on my knees and scream in your face to *please, take me back*. i grasp your shriveled wrists and shake them violently so as to disturb the quiet of nighttime itself. and amidst choking on desperate shrieks i widen my open mouth a little further in an attempt to consume your face. like a female spider, the final lovemaking in the story of us would be the ingestion of your body.

but just at the height of my neurotic outburst, i reach an epiphany. the monster under my bed isn't you. it isn't the *you* i fell in love with. it is nothing more than a mere holographic memory burned into my cerebrum, replaying over and over you telling me that you've fallen out of love. it is every insecurity i ever had in our relationship now a reality. i understand now that i do not want the version of you that does not want me. i do not want who you are now or what you have become. i want the boy i fell in love with, not the young man who raped me. but i realize that, in the end, they are the same person. and that boy i love doesn't exist anymore except in my own memory.

and so the wilted wrists fade into nothingness as i realize my fingernails are digging into my palms. and i am once again alone: the way you intended. caught in the act: an atheist kneeling at her bedside. *and so, i give in.* still kneeling, i interlock all ten of my bony fingers and i pray. i pray that maybe, in the morning, i will feel okay again.

i do not want silence.
nothing in my life is silent.
my thoughts are loud;
if you are too quiet,
i will not be able to hear your voice
over the voices in my head.
(they are inconsiderate that way).
and so if you must leave
(and by god, i wish you wouldn't)
if you must leave, *leave me loudly.*
i want crying and shouting;
do not vanish into a ghost
and haunt me in the night.
hold me tightly
and love me loudly
leave me loudly
put your guns up;
there must be n o i s e
there will be n o i s e
n o i s e , n o i s e , n o i s e !

and he never liked handcuffs anyway, so why would i wish those upon him? i would never want that. i want for him what he wanted for me. crying into the toilet on a thursday afternoon following the dreaded devil's dance. the dance only one out of two people wanted. locking yourself in the bathroom, heaving so hard you throw up. wishing it had been blood instead. but you've cried yourself dry.

not the physicality, but i wish that sadness for him. and i hope it is all because of me. i hope i'm the reason he regrets everything.

—this is my anger talking

frère jacques, frère jacques
are you asleep?

frère jacques, frère jacques
where do you go when you dream?

my life is a balancing act in twelve-hour intervals. i spend almost all hours of daylight being unconscious, passed out, brain-dead, for lack of better words. but he made me afraid of the dark. i have become nocturnal: dearest *insomniac*. and all twenty-four hours, i am dead to the world, regardless of whether my eyes are open or shut. in some ways, a part of me is always asleep. because certain parts of my brain have blocked out large chunks of my memory and sent my mind into autopilot. i am numb to the world. i take burning showers just to feel something. i am to the degree of tiredness that i feel perfectly comfortable laying on hard bathroom tiles; the weight of existence is too heavy to carry. i often forget to eat and drink. half of the time i am passed out, and the other half i am wishing i was. i live alone and function unintentionally mute; sometimes i scream just to see if i still can. i once heard the term *somnambulist*. it means 'sleepwalker'. and all the while i float in a world that feels out of place, somehow this word feels like it fits. because i am a walking sleep disorder. i am dead to the world. i am not awake when i appear to be and yet i am never fully asleep. i am simultaneously both a narcoleptic and an insomniac. i exist in an in-between state of consciousness only achievable through great trauma.

you found me at my darkest
oh, you were my moon

but alas,

you did not stick around
to see the sunrise.

i gave my soul to you
and by the time you left me,
i had no idea who i was anymore.

cry out
your love drops.

i am sorry you hurt
from things
you can't talk about.

i think we sleep a lot
when we are sad
because it is a coping mechanism.
our bodies are trying to save us
from our own minds.

it is okay if some days
all you can muster
the courage to do

is sleep.

and finally, this is the part
unexpected, like the beginning
but this time, in a better way:

i never expected
i would be the one
to heal me
in the end.

and the truth is, i'm not fully healed.
but this is me documenting
the beginning of the process.

these are just some thoughts
i have had while traveling
the roads of recovery
but there are many, many
miles before me still…

where does love begin? asked the therapist. well, i thought it started when i met him. began with a shy glance that turned to giggling smiles and, soon enough, hands meeting and two bodies interlocking to become one. and it ended in him leaving me alone and needing therapy. *no,* said the therapist. *try again.* okay, love starts here. alone, in therapy. in healing. love begins with me. and every person i decide to add to that love is simply an asset. there is and has been love all along, even as 'ours' was falling apart. there is one love that nobody should ever have the ability to steal from me: my love for myself. *now you have the right idea,* said the therapist.

my therapist has always told me: *never stop loving.* even if people hurt you. people will let you down. do not give up hope that there are good people in the world. donate when you have something to give. volunteer when you are hurting most. and do not stop searching for people who deserve to be in your life. because if you keep on loving, love will find you. and the right ones will stay.

—the secret to being loved is to love first

and what if
you never find a soulmate?
what if you never get the chance
to be married? then what will you do?

the answer: heal.

oh, the number of times
i have woken up my parents
screaming in my sleep
we laugh it off
it was a bad dream
but the thing is
they don't know
what goes on
inside my head

—ptsd

when will i learn?
that it takes more effort
to ridicule my existence
than it does to accept
my own imperfection.

i thought i found love in you
but in your absence
i found in myself
something better: a home

i am not broken or ill
sure, anxious and depressed;

i am complicated,
intricate, and beautiful.

—mind's eye

we are not broken or shattered
despite sharp edges
red in the corners
god is making stained glass

—mosaic

i have always tried to lose weight.
to make myself smaller.
but then i lost you.
and then *the weight of you*
was gone from my life.
the rock that had been burdening my shoulders:
disappeared.
and suddenly, i realized
that minus you, *i feel lighter*.
and ever since then,
i have never needed to make myself smaller.
i am a bigger, happier soul without you.

and what people don't tell you is that healing involves more grieving than you would expect. grieving for your old self: the girl you once were. mourning everything that has ever left you. a burning hate in your stomach for the damn impermanence of it all. but everything you lose is one step toward finding yourself; reminding you over and over again that you must be able to count on yourself. you must fall in love with the process of allowing yourself to grieve in productive ways: and to make peace with the things that haunt you.

…for from the two extremes:
two mountains, and between
my open legs one can find
a hidden valley. too good
but not good enough.
where i am from, we do not
climb mountains, but attempt
to live between them.

come out little phoenix,
i will name you *fire*.
try not to get caught
in the rings of barbed wire
about my privates.

i'd pour my flesh and blood
into this small creature
hoping that i could
teach her to be happy
in a way that i was never able
to achieve for myself.

—if this made a baby

and on that point
it is almost like
the universe conspired
to collect your atoms
into this home of a body
so that you just might
learn to love yourself
in a way that your mother
could not love herself.

—the butterfly effect

the chaos
of the universe
is contained
between my legs

—stardust

for a long time, i considered myself his one-that-got-away. the great girl who he ignorantly broke up with and will never get back. the breakup he will always look back on with regret. but really? in reality, i wasn't a great girl to him. i was young and dumb. i was, as they call *sophomores*: a wise fool. i was broken inside and out, i was manipulative and extremely emotional. i was anxiously attached and codependent with him. for god's sake, i cheated on him. i retaliated; broke his trust as he broke mine. and i did it with sex. i recognize all of that now. but being older still, i admit such things while maintaining with complete certainty that none of that warranted him raping me. sex can easily be made a weapon, but he made it a gun. i did not deserve that; nobody does. i did not ask for that; nobody would. and it never was and never will be justified.

love yourself
if for no other reason
as a form of revenge
against everyone
who has ever tried
to convince you not to

why look up at a sky full of stars
if not to feel wonder at all the possibilities
that you never could have lived;
the statistical infinity of possibilities
that each speck of dust making up our planets
would settle in such a way
that your existence was made possible.

and yet,
despite infinite doubt:
here you are.

—the illusion

and the stars?
why, they remind us:

we can shine
even in darkness.

is the darkness
what makes the night, night?

do the stars not shine through it,
each one of them simply a more distant sun?

for so long i have wept and wilted
at lost loves and what-could-have-beens.

but i finally see it now: i must run forward.
i look, and there is light.

my bedside lampshade
floods my room
with apricot light
honey rays, yellow blossom
glowing like a dim star
amidst cold shadows

                              —you keep away my demons

but oh, to once be a prisoner of your heart. the person you loved so violently: your hands on me, i was crushed under the weight of everything you are. and me? i am the one you broke up with because you could not handle the wrath of my resentment. but you know what? i am still a prisoner. even long after you have disappeared from my life; you have not disappeared from my mind. you are dead to me; yet i keep raising the dead by writing these damn books. dusting off the ungodly: the past. you are dead to me in a your-spirit-haunts-me kind of way. and essentially? because of you, i am now a prisoner of my own mind.

—post-traumatic stress

somewhere outside right now
the clouds are dark and warm;
so many water particles
packed as densely
as neurons in a human brain
to form miles and miles
of thick, foggy quilting
beneath which all of
the fatigued and weary
may effortlessly
             sink

                  sink

                     sink

into a dark and warm

                                      sleep.

you used to hold me
the nights i was so depressed
i cried myself to sleep

but now that you're gone
the funny part is
i sleep soundly without you

—peace

the hollow pang in my stomach
and familiar friend insomnia
somehow feel like a relief.
a gift, even. for i used to
question, on nights like this,
whether i was alive at all.
but after it all, i know now:
because my thoughts exist
(despite how dark they are)
so must i. and he said:
i think, therefore i exist.

i don't feel as though
my head is swimming
in honey anymore;

it's more of a thin syrup now…

—progress

it has been
a glorious fight

;

still is.

truly becoming an adult
is simply rediscovering
your childhood personality.

your interests and dreams;
before the world tried
to corrupt you.

before all you ever wanted
was to be older:
and finally, you are.

and it never required
much learning,
only unlearning.

—growing up

if you ever feel *alone*
with the person you *love*

run. run. run. *run.*

and what do we do
when times get tough?

we push until
the bone bleeds

and even then
we grow a new one.

who are we?
we are the girls
who built ourselves
from the ground-up
out of the sticks and stones
they threw at us.

you left me
don't miss me?

i will sweat so hard i swear
and i will grow and better myself

until i am sure
that you do.

until you go mad.
and the last laugh is

that after you leave me once
i am gone forever.

i regret letting you leave me. i needed to leave *you*. i had to be on my own and find myself. i forged myself into a woman from the hot fires of high school hells. emerging from scorched coals (pieces of my heart) i rise as a phoenix. i have learned self-respect. i have reflected countless hours upon the toxicity you provided in my life as you spoon-fed me lies. like how i am not pretty enough to be wanted by anyone else. or that my mental illness makes me unlovable. but there are days i sit around and miss the ignorant bliss of it all. the days before you punctured my soul. the friendship blossoming into a youthful romance, years before i knew how hard life really was. i miss the night we kissed in the rain, even if it will never happen again. if anyone ever asked me if i miss you, i would say no. because i don't. *i miss me.* i miss the younger version of myself that was innocent enough to trust overconfident young men. and still, navigating the dark trenches of adult life, i wish i could run to you and the arms that were my home at one point in time: when i was young.

if i could say one thing uninterrupted to my ex-boyfriend, i think i would say nothing. of course, i hope he has a dreadful day the day he learns of this book. and i hope i'm the reason. i hope he hates how much i have grown since he knew me. the best revenge is proving to him that i am no longer the girl he once knew; *the girl he raped: she no longer exists*. and i hope that my words punctuate where it hurts. but honestly? i don't need any of that. he needs that; that is why he is who he is. i need not stoop to his level. because i do not start things, but i finish them quietly and with kindness.

—i am the bigger person.

i am sorry
somebody loved you
so violently
that you learned
to equate pain
with validation.
please know
that they never loved you.
you must unlearn.
and you must know:
you never deserved that.

the universe did not conspire
to collect your atoms
into this home of a body
just for you to tear it down
in mourning for everything
that has ever left you

you deserve more than that

and the bouquets i had kept sacred
in memory of our love:

i dried the roses carefully
then burnt them to the ground

in a chemical fire.
and i scattered the ashes of us

on rain-soaked,
parking-lot pavement.

i found god that evening
and i was her.

—good riddance

to be insistent,

this is not the happy ending;
i don't even know if there is one,
but that is another book.

this is where i have
accepted what happened to me.
no, i am not fully healed.
i live every day
with ptsd and sleep troubles.

but i am okay with that for now.

i can move on,
but i have not forgotten.
and i never will.

with love,
the hopeful somnambulist

about the author

Taryn Riddle is a young American poet interested in mental illness and wellness. Taryn was raised in Bolton, Massachusetts and practiced daily journaling from the time she could first hold a pencil through her early college years. Her writing is inspired by personal struggles and life experiences. At the time of this publication, she resides in Boston, Massachusetts and is a recent college graduate with a bachelor's of science in behavioral neuroscience and philosophy. Taryn is active on social media, most notably on Instagram @tarynriddlee.

All illustrations for this book are by Taryn Riddle.

dedication

for anyone who is afraid to fall asleep.

i hope that in reading this book
you may feel less alone.